FoR DoRIS —

DIE TO LIVE:

To the Edge of Heaven and Back

ALOHA KE AKUA,

Gordon Norio

Happy Birthday Enjoy! ♡ Ann

DIE TO LIVE:

To the Edge of Heaven and Back

First American Paperback Edition
ISBN-13: 978-0-9991624-2-2
ISBN-10: 099916242X
LCCN: 2018901760

Cover design: Caligraphics

4

TABLE OF CONTENTS

AKNOWLEDGEMENTS

First and foremost, I give thanks and all glory to the most high God, Yaweh, Elohim; our Lord and Savior Christ Jesus / Yeshua HaMashiach, the Name above all names; the Holy Spirit aka Ruach HaKodesh: Every breath, every idea, every pen stroke, every moment, I dedicate to you.

To my wife, Iwalani: You are the one God chose for me to live, love, and laugh with.

To Auntie Rowena Sargent: Your input and memories served as an invaluable contribution to this story.

NUMBERS 6:24-26

INTRODUCTION

The supernatural is challenging to describe in writing. It can be just as demanding to convey it in the spoken word. The majority of us learn most effectively with images– perhaps that is why the film and television industry has such a powerful impact on how and what we think.

The time and effort I put into writing this story was not difficult. I am not expressing false humility when I say that; I merely recorded the basic facts as told to me by Virginia and others. What made this process arduous is that Virginia had a difficult time articulating her Heavenly encounters. Her mother insisted that she never speak of these things so Virginia suppressed much of it. How was I to write about them?

The amazing answer arrived after asking God to help me apply this into book form. As I presented the sections to Virginia for review, she was shocked by the accuracy of how I described her near-death encounters. More than once, she wept and told me, "That's exactly how it happened! How did you know?"

I didn't. God did. He told me what to write. I remained in obedience to the guidance given to me by the Holy Spirit.

This book is based on real life events. The prologue is the result of my research of the catastrophe in southern Italy that brought Virginia's father, Domenico, to America. Some names throughout the story were changed or fabricated.

Scientists may argue that there is no empirical evidence regarding near-death experiences. I would contend that the supernatural is far more real than what our limited five senses can detect. Quantum physics and life in the Spirit are finding more common ground every day. It is my prayer that in the very near future, the two will merge to help us understand what *reality* truly means.

PROLOGUE

28 December, 1908 5:20 a.m.

Tiriolo Catanzaro, Calabria Province, Italy

The bed was shaking. 16 year-old Domenico Renda was accustomed to the pranks of his siblings. This morning, however, felt different. For one, it was very early. Still dark out. Given the Christmas holiday, school would not resume for another few days. The shaking increased as Domenico heard glass breaking in the kitchen. The earthquake that had rattled

Calabria a little over three years ago still brought nightmares and was more of a swaying motion; this morning, the house was starting to move violently up and down.

As he rolled out of bed, Domenico struggled to stay on his feet, as the house seemed to move in every direction at once. He heard a scream from his parent's bedroom. Terror and adrenaline hit him simultaneously while he made his way to the front door of the house. A vase crashed to the floor, trying to block his escape. The small tea table at the entrance to the modest home was assaulting him while he opened the door, retreating from the onslaught.

14

More screams could be heard in the village over the loud rumble of what would later be known as the most devastating earthquake in Europe's history.

Domenico experienced the next moments in slow motion. Watching the home he was born in collapse, followed by his best friend's house next door, then other houses started to fall like dominoes. The ground moved like sloshing liquid as the boy struggled for a firm footing. Four houses down, toward the center of town, a fire broke out and quickly began to engulf wood, straw, food, furniture, and the inhabitants of Tiriolo Catanzaro. It felt as though the earth mercilessly heaved for hours, when in reality it was over in thirty seconds. Then the real nightmare began.

With each subsequent aftershock, Domenico's terror increased. His family was gone as were most of the people he had known all of his young life. What began as a light drizzle was now a steady rain. Domenico heard a cracking sound across the valley from his now leveled village and watched a massive swath of hillside melt into a landslide that took massive trees, boulders, and the odd farmhouse into the ravine. Looking around in every direction, all the young man could see was death and devastation.

After two days, the stench of decaying bodies was nauseating. The survivors had done all they could to rescue those trapped in the rubble. Dogs, cats, rats, and crows were picking at the corpses that were not yet buried, so great was the number lost. One couple, with whom Domenico was acquainted but did not know vey well, asked him where his family was. Domenico started to shake and the tears started to flow as he explained they were all lost. The husband and wife, whose two children were buried when their house collapsed, told him they were going to the main city of Reggio Calabria where they would take a ferry to Messina. Asking if he would care to join them, Domenico surveyed the crushed remains of all he knew. With a handful of Lire, an extra shirt and pair of pants, and his mandolin in a scarred leather case, the teenager walked out of the village between the grieving man and woman whose names he could not remember.

As the three travelers approached Reggio Calabria four days later, they faced a number of people leaving the city. Sad, dejected, looking at the ground as they left by the hundreds, the couple tried asking people what was happening to no avail. As they crested the hill overlooking the city, they could see it had been obliterated. A forty-foot tsunami had ravaged both Reggio Calabria and the port city of Messina across the straits. No solace would be found here. A dirty-uniformed carabinieri suggested they go to Messina, where King Victor Emmanuel III had arrived two days before and was ordering the execution of looters and the evacuation of refugees. Navy ships from France, Great Britain, and the United States were assisting in the relief. Because Domenico had relatives in the U.S., he found himself aboard the *USS Celtic*, an American supply ship ferrying survivors to Naples for relocation or emigration. Due to his small stature, most people assumed he was ten or eleven years of age and kept a protective eye on the traumatized boy. An official of the Province of Napoli assigned Domenico to the cargo ship *Florida*, which would take him and eight hundred fifty other southern Italians to Boston, Massachusetts to make a new home in a new land. Lost in a dense fog, the *Florida* collided with the luxury passenger liner *Republic*. Three people aboard the *Florida* were killed instantly. Within minutes, pandemonium broke out on the ship. Angelo Ruspini, captain of the *Florida,* used extreme measures to regain control of the desperate passengers, including firing gunshots into the air. Eventually the survivors were rescued at sea and brought into Boston Harbor where they would start a new life.

CHAPTER 1. The American Dream

1909 - 1939

Domenico was processed through Boston and given the standard WOP tag pinned to his jacket. At that time, WOP was not a derogatory term; it simply meant "Without Papers". The boy had yet to contact either of his two brothers. With very little money and one change of clothes, Domenico was destined to a life on the streets. He noticed an older man playing a violin on the sidewalk with the instrument's case open at his feet. This inspired the boy to walk a few blocks away, open up his case, and play the mandolin he brought on the journey. It wasn't long before enough money had accumulated in the case to get a good meal and a new pair of shoes.

Domenico had two older brothers living there, who had migrated to the states years earlier. He wrote a brief letter in Italian, stating his intention to join them. His eldest brother instructed Domenico to take the train ride and wait for him at the Haymarket Station. After two days of sitting at the main entrance, Domenico knew his brother would not be coming for him. He opened up his mandolin case, tuned the strings, and began playing. A tall man in uniform approached him and asked, "Are you an American citizen?"

Domenico froze, not sure how to answer. He had already seen the scorn heaped upon immigrants in the city and was prepared for the worst.

"Do you *want* to be an American citizen?" the soldier inquired.

Domenico felt a sense of relief and excitement as he nodded silently.

"Come with me then."

The teenager followed on the heels of the soldier as he swaggered to an office around the corner. The officer pushed papers in front of the young man to sign. Domenico handed the papers back to the officer who smiled wryly, saying, "Welcome to the United States Army, son."

In the seventh week of basic training, Domenico was assigned to demolitions to learn how to handle TNT, defuse hand grenades, and wire detonators. In spite of strict safety protocol, accidents would happen on occasion. Domenico had his back turned to another soldier who was wiring a detonator behind a steel-plated wall, designed to buffer any mishaps. Unfortunately, the bolts that held the plate to the outdoor concrete pad were rusty. The soldier crossed the wires - the explosion blew the steel plate off its mount, hitting Domenico in the back. The only thing that saved his life was the fact that he was bent over, which spared his skull from being caved in; nonetheless, the injuries to his back put Domenico in hospital and consequently he was discharged from service with a Purple Heart and a lifetime of pain.

With what little he had saved from his brief time in the Army, Domenico bought a used Triumph motorcycle, complete with saddlebags, and began riding the countryside in search of a place he could call home. Domenico had an innate skill for tinkering with mechanical items. At a young age, his father gave him old watches, which the boy would take apart and put back together effortlessly. In Calabria, Domenico's neighbors would bring their broken watches, and looked on in amazement, as the young lad would repair them in record time. This skill served him well on the highways of America- anytime the temperamental Triumph would act up, a couple turns of a wrench in his hands would have the bike up and running again.

Domenico's father was also the local shoemaker in their village. He taught his son the intricacies of building saddles or a pair of shoes or boots. It was not unusual for people from neighboring villages to make the trek to Tiriolo Catanzaro for the senior Renda's well-crafted footwear. Italy's reputation for quality shoes was due to craftsmen that put tremendous care and attention to detail into their work. Domenico knew his mechanical and trade skills imparted to him by his father would provide opportunities wherever he decided to call home. Before he found that place, he discovered something else that would capture his fancy.

Bessie McCoy Newton was born in in 1892 in Nebraska underneath a pioneer-driven westbound Contestoga covered wagon and raised in Oklahoma. Today found her hunched over her sewing machine working on a dress in the tiny hamlet of Harlowtown, Montana (Population: 651). Her back was aching, not so much from the long days she spent on her projects; the pain was working its way up and down her spine from where her back had been broken, the by-product of an abusive marriage to a violent, drunken husband. She had fled her first marriage because of the man's cruelty and had no idea that her second relationship would turn out even worse. Both men were Italian, alcoholic, and irresistibly handsome. Bessie had learned to speak fluent Italian from her first husband, although most of their conversations were shouting matches. To date, she had six children from her first marriage, two of which died at birth. Bessie had four more children with her current husband, and tragically, one of them had died at birth also. The emotional scars of death and abuse had not worn on her beauty; she still turned heads wherever she went. And today was no exception as she stepped out of the back room where she did her sewing for some fresh air. Bessie looked up at a cloudless sky, the brightness of the sun causing her to squint. The afternoon heat was gathering clouds far to the northwest over the mountains; it wouldn't be long before an evening shower would roll in and unleash some much needed rain. Bessie stepped off the porch and walked toward the street, wondering what the approaching thunderous racket was. Her adventurous spirit lit up as Domenico rolled into the neighborhood; his eye for beauty had him steer the bike to the edge of the unpaved road right next to Bessie. He killed the engine and lifted his goggles.

"Scusami, signorina, uh, miss…" Domenico said with a flashing smile. That's all Bessie needed to hear.

"What can I do for you?" she inquired, in a flirting tone.

"I look for the way around the lago, how you say, the lake, ah, to Jawbone Creek."

Bessie looked northeast and pointed. "First, you have to go to the end of this road, make a left, and keep going till you see the lake. Turn left and follow the shoreline all the way to the creek. That's a lovely motorcycle," she said, admiring the rider more than the ride.

"Maybe you like a ride?"

"Maybe. How do I know I'm safe with you?"

"I'm a gentleman, signorina. I'm a knight; this-a my horse."

Bessie giggled. She looked over her shoulder at the shop and the pile of work inside.

"Allora portami a fare un giro, signore coraggioso!" (*Then take me for a ride, brave sir!*), she announced in perfect Italian as she curtsied. It was the last time she saw Harlowtown as she climbed on the back of the Triumph, wrapping her arms around Domenico's waist.

After a whirlwind divorce, Bessie and Domenico had a quickie marriage with a justice of the peace officiating in Billings. The newlyweds made their way east, touring through North Dakota and Minnesota, making it as far as Milwaukee, Wisconsin.

As they turned south into Illinois, they backtracked through the rolling cornfields of Iowa and Nebraska. They turned north at Cheyenne, making their way to the Shoshone National Forest and Yellowstone National Park. They were awestruck by the beauty of the land and the abundance of wildlife. The sky went on forever in all directions. Continuing north, they went as far as Medicine Hat in Canada, then turned south once again to return to the states at Havre, Montana. Heading east, as they rode into the tiny town of Chinook, Domenico stopped the Triumph and shut off the motor. A short row of low-lying storefronts, each with its own unique façade, lined the main street. Two men on horseback ambled by, their horses lazily kicking up a little dust as the cowboys nodded with a tip of their hats. Dom looked over his shoulder at Bessie and they nodded to each other with mutual smiles, silently agreeing they were home.

Bessie picked up sewing projects as Domenico laid the foundation for building a saddlery and shoemaker business. He had his eye on a corner lot near the southwest end of town and declared to himself and his bride that he would build the biggest, best house in Chinook. Although saddles, boots, and shoes were in steady demand, Domenico picked up another skill that far surpassed the income brought in from his shoemaker abilities: Dom became one of the best poker players for miles around. Within two years of their combined efforts, Domenico and Bessie had saved enough money to pay for the house in full. Lacking faith in the banking system, he literally socked away the funds. When they finalized the deal, Dom handed over stockings full of cash; the shock on both the faces of the property owner and the builder gave the couple something to giggle about for years to come.

All of Dom's and Bessie's children were delivered by a midwife except for the youngest. Mrs. Kirkhoven was very special in the community and loved and respected by everyone. She was from Scotland and had clubfeet but she never let it bother her.

Domenico and Bessie bartered for almost everything except gas and electricity for the house. Every time a baby was born, Mrs. Kirkhoven received a new pair of custom shoes built by Dom. Because her feet were so terribly deformed, Mrs. Kirkhoven came to rely on the fertile

Rendas for shoes. Which each subsequent birth, her collection expanded to include pink felt ones for weddings; black for funerals, and other colors to match her clothes. Domenico was a genius at making specialized shoes for the woman's deformed feet. Mrs. Kirkhoven, a registered nurse, was a survivor of the Titanic and would regale the family with stories of "the boat ride she would never forget."

Their first son, William Domenico, was born in the house on the southwest side of town. The saddlery and shoe store took up most of the lower part of the house, with a back room that would become young William's nursery and later the bedroom for his siblings. Two years later, Rowena Mae was born, then Lucille Rae, followed by Evelyn Virginia. Mrs. Kirkhoven did not deliver the last Renda baby because he was extra large and Bessie's age was a factor. For safety's sake, they traveled twenty-one miles to the hospital in Havre. In spite of the child's size and other complications, the youngest Renda came into the world healthy– and quietly, a characteristic he would possess throughout his life. The obstetrician, Dr. O'Malley, had no children of his own. He insisted that the boy be named "Patrick", since he was born on St. Patrick's Day. Domenico would have none of it, retorting that no Italian boy should be named Patrick. Dr. O'Malley delayed giving the Rendas a birth certificate until Bessie said to her husband, "Dom, we must have a birth certificate for this baby."

Domenico relented, making it official: Joseph Patrick Renda was their fifth and final child.

Bessie felt blessed that in spite of the extreme winters in Montana, all of her children with Dom survived in an era of twenty-five percent infant mortality rate; however, an unexpected storm lay on the horizon.

From the start, Virginia, their fourth child, was a headstrong little girl. Virginia's older brother and sisters were doting siblings; between them and Bessie, Virginia's feet scarcely touched the ground. Her bright blue eyes and rambunctious behavior were endearing traits that kept the family amused with her antics.

In May, on her fifth birthday, Virginia's parents walked her to Mrs. Sondheim's house. Helga Sondheim was a concert pianist of the finest caliber. Recently widowed, she made ends meet by teaching piano. Tall and lean, with wisps of gray in her dark blonde hair, Mrs. Sondheim held a stern countenance which at first intimidated Virginia; however, as they became more acquainted, the young girl saw the same stubborn streak in her mentor that she carried. Helga treated Virginia like her own daughter and the relationship led Virginia to become a virtuoso in piano, a skill she practiced and later passed on to hundreds of students throughout her lifetime.

The first cold front of the season swept down from Canada earlier than usual. Virginia got a sore throat, which was not uncommon with a sudden change in the weather. Always on the go, the young girl resisted bed rest and the sore throat became a case of *Streptococcus*, or strep throat. Nobody noticed that her fever increased as the infection began moving into Virginia's bloodstream; the first noticeable symptoms

45

were a red, bumpy rash covering her back and a "strawberry tongue", classic indicators for scarlet fever. Without rest, further complications set in. Within four days, Virginia's poor immune response led to ear and sinus infections, followed by full-blown sepsis. On the seventh day, by the time her oldest sister noticed how bad things had become, her fever spiked to one hundred four degrees. Bessie put her daughter in bed, called the local doctor, and waited.

The frail five-year-old was in critical condition when Dr. O'Malley arrived at the house. Being the only physician in the vicinity, O'Malley's duties included all the citizens of Chinook: Humans, dogs, cats, horses, sheep, goats, and cattle. With a full schedule most days, his bedside manner was sorely lacking; the country doctor gave Virginia a cursory exam, looked at the worried mother, and said, "Bessie, better prepare for a funeral", then walked out the door.

Bessie brought in a pastor to deliver the last rites. The two began to pray at the foot of the bed where Virginia was tossing about restlessly. Suddenly, she became very still. The girl, who had been vacillating between aches, chills, sweating, and convulsions, felt a sense of peace, which started in her body, then settled in her mind. All discomfort and worry left her as her body began to feel extremely light. As the physical weight decreased, Virginia sensed herself rising off of the bed and became aware of being able to see in every direction at once. The walls and ceiling of the house became translucent. The prayers of the pastor caught her attention and she could even hear his thoughts layered beneath the prayers– the tiny day-to-day distractions intruding upon his petitions to God. Virginia could hear the internal dialogue of her mother, pleading to the Lord to make her child well again.

Suddenly, Virginia felt a pull, as if the top of her head was on a string. The pull wasn't uncomfortable but it was continuous, asking to pull her upward but only if Virginia gave it permission to do so. This concept wasn't spelled out in words but the young girl could comprehend it. As she acquiesced to the pull, mentally saying *'yes'*, Virginia instantly found herself streaking upward, away from the scene she was hovering over. The noise became deafening, as if she were standing right next to the tracks as a train sped by. The rush of wind blew her hair back and even though it appeared as if her entire body was traveling, she looked down and, in what appeared to be hundreds of miles away, could still see herself lying on the sweat-stained sheets as her mother and the pastor held vigil.

Virginia sensed that a major destination lay ahead; as if that train was about to pull into the station; however, before it arrived, she had another concept download into her mind, almost hearing it as an audible voice but as if it were speaking inside of her: "It is not your time yet." In an instant, she was freefalling, down toward her body, the wind howling inside the pipeline leading back to her physical self. With a loud *snap*, Virginia was back in her physical frame, feeling the heaviness of gravity, the heat of fever, the ache of muscles, the beating of her heart. As the pastor placed his hand on her forehead, he was the first to notice that her fever appeared to be breaking. He looked to the worried mother and said, "Bessie, I do believe our prayers have been answered."

Virginia slept peacefully through the remainder of the afternoon and the entire night. As the magpies began cawing at dawn, the young girl opened her eyes to see her mother dozing in the chair next to the bed. Bessie heard the little girl stirring and opened her exhausted eyes.

"Thank heavens. Virginia, we've been so worried about you." Hearing their mother's voice, one by one, the child's brothers and sisters cautiously filed in from the rooms down the hall they shared.

"Mother, I was floating in the air and saw you and Reverend Collier."

"You were probably just dreaming, hon." Bessie turned to the children looking at their recovering sibling. In a kind, soft voice, she instructed the other children, "Rowena, go get breakfast started. Your sister is probably starving. You ready to eat, Virginia?"

The little girl nodded from the bed.

"That's good. The rest of you go help your sister with breakfast and get your chores done."

As the children moved down the hallway toward the kitchen, Bessie turned to her daughter. "You said you were floating in the air; was there anything else?"

Virginia replied, "Yes, Mother. I saw you and Pastor praying and then a voice called me to heaven. I followed it and I could see all around me. I could see Rowena, and Joe, and everybody– I looked down and could see the whole town as I went up. I even saw Farmer Miller's horse stretching her neck through the fence to get a bite of grass!" Virginia was giddy with excitement. "Then an angel told me I had to come back because God wasn't ready for me yet. I fell a long ways until I got back in my body and woke up."

Bessie looked at her daughter with a stern look on her face. "Virginia," she said in a tone reserved for extreme punishment, "Don't let me EVER hear you talk about floating in the air again or going to heaven or any of that nonsense. You'll have the whole town in an uproar and they'll think you're a witch or a devil or worse. You don't want that, do you?"

"No Mother, but it was so real…"

Bessie hissed at the young girl. "I said never, Evelyn Virginia! If I ever hear of this again, I will tell your father and he will beat the tar out of you!"

Virginia recovered and was left with poststreptococcal glomerulonephritis, which permanently damaged her kidneys in a minor way. Two other long-term effects were hearing impairment, which gradually increased throughout her life and a vulnerability to spinal meningitis. Beyond that, she had a typical mid-western American life, growing up in a community of caring, connected citizens.

CHAPTER 2. The American Nightmare

1940 - 1950

Big Sky Country

Chinook, Montana is on the prairie where the wind howls in winter, sending snow into huge drifts that sometimes are high enough to tunnel through. Any exposed skin feels the sting of the snow until the frosty air numbs the vulnerable tissue. Not a friendly place to be in winter.

Following the attack on Pearl Harbor in 1941, most people of Japanese descent, even second and third generation American citizens were considered suspect. Land and businesses were seized without due process. The majority lived in the western states of Oregon, Washington, California, and the territory of Hawaii. Internment camps were built in remote areas, surrounded by barbed wire, where many families were "relocated". The worst irony in this scenario was that young U.S. soldiers of Japanese descent were allowed to visit their families in these concentration camps on American soil.

It was a tragic time for the Sasaki and Sagami families: they were torn from their truck farm in Orting, Washington. Chinook was one locale where the United States Government forced these and other families to be imprisoned for the duration of the war. They were sent to farms to live in worker housing, which were little more than shacks designed for use during harvest season, not the bitter cold of winter. More than a few illegally incarcerated souls were lost in the freezing conditions. Due to the distance, snowdrifts, and cold, the Japanese children were unable to attend school. Other families of the community took compassion on them and began to invite the children to stay in their homes during the school months. The Sasaki and Sagami children stayed with the

Renda clan. The cross-cultures of Italian and Japanese led to unique learning experiences for both families, the Japanese kids discovering how to eat spaghetti and the Rendas learning to eat with chopsticks. The young Sagami and Sasaki girls learned sewing from Bessie, who taught them how to make elegant clothes. This acceptance and adoption of sorts made these displaced young girls feel wanted, appreciated, and gave them a sense of purpose. The kindness was extended both ways, making for lifelong friendships that exist to this day.

Because many of the farmers in and around Chinook were of German ancestry, the German prisoners of war were also brought into the region. Due to the cold and remoteness, the Army had no concern that these POWs would run away; in fact, they had no reason or desire to escape. Compared to the conditions these former German soldiers fought in, life in Chinook was abundant with food, basic comforts– and some of the locals spoke their language. POWs running errands into town, milking cows, and sharing in other basic chores became commonplace. The biggest irony in this scenario was that young U.S. soldiers of Japanese descent were allowed to visit their families in concentration camps on American soil.

In addition to the immigrants and prisoners, some Germans fled their homeland when it was apparent that the Nazi regime would destroy their way of life. One of the refugees, John Siert, was a carpenter who brought his sister and her daughter with him to America. He asked Virginia if she would teach his niece, Maria, English. Virginia was excited at the prospect and connected immediately with Maria. Both girls were fourteen, yet Maria, with long blonde hair, blue eyes, and dimples, towered over Virginia. The two worked hard to get to know and understand each other.

As time passed, Virginia came to learn that Maria was a product of Hitler's Master Race experiments. She never knew her father: Maria's mother was forcibly impregnated by a man she neither knew nor loved. Maria showed pictures of herself in Hitler Youth uniform with a Swastika armband and once demonstrated how she was trained to march.

"EIN, ZWEI, DREI, VIER!"

Virginia was horrified as she watched her friend metamorphose from the quiet, reserved young girl she knew into a cold, menacing product of an evil, corrupt empire. She never asked Maria to speak of her childhood again although the girls remained friends until Maria moved away to the East after the war.

July 4th, 1946 promised to be extra special with a grand community picnic in Chinook. Plenty of steak from the ranches, fried chicken, massive potatoes from nearby Idaho loaded with butter and sour cream, Nebraska corn with more butter, cole slaw, biscuits (and butter), and pies of every flavor would be laid out on a long table. The war had ended over one year ago and celebration in America seemed to be constant. The economy was booming, now that rationing had discontinued and the population was on the upswing with plenty of young men back from combat– and women who had been lonely during the war years. It was as if there was a marriage every day of the week along with subsequent "We're having a baby!" announcements going out. Manufacturing, farming, engineering, home construction– the boom time was moving into full swing.

That summer proved to be hotter than usual and with school on vacation, families flocked to the nation's rivers, lakes, and swimming pools for a cool respite. And while these waters gave relief from the heat, the volume of people brought an invisible menace to anyone who entered the water. It was two days after taking a swim that Virginia was enjoying an early ride on her bicycle. She was excited about the upcoming picnic with food, music...and boys. As she pedaled in the cool morning, she began to feel warmer than normal and her back began to ache. By the time she turned for home, Virginia had to stop, get off her bicycle, and vomit. Sweat trickled down her spine. When she reached the steps of the family home, her neck was so stiff she could not turn her head from side to side. A pounding between her temples felt like a hammer hitting her skull. She left the bike by the front steps and went straight to her bedroom to lie down.

Later in the day, Rowena, Virginia's oldest sister, checked in on her sibling. When she observed that Virginia was tossing and turning with a high fever, Rowena ran to get her boyfriend Victor and asked him to drive them to the hospital. As they were leaving, Rowena took Domenico aside to tell him what was happening.

"Father, Virginia needs to see a doctor. Victor and I are taking her to the hospital. As soon as I know anything, I will come home and let you and Mother know about it."

Domenico replied, "You a good girl to look after your sister. You go."

By the time they reached the hospital, Virginia's fever was tipping past one hundred five degrees. The admitting staff had standing orders to refuse anyone suspected of having polio. Young Virginia was no exception; the outbreak was well publicized and the staff had seen enough cases to know who to admit and who to send away. Rowena and Victor had no choice but to return home. When Domenico saw them walking back in the house with Virginia in Victor's arms, he was perplexed.

"What's-a this about?"

"They won't admit her, Father," Rowena said dejectedly. "They think she has polio."

Domenico was furious, his eyes narrowed. Slowly and deliberately, he pointed to Victor as he spoke in a quiet voice. "You take my girl, and put her back in the car. I gonna come with you."

Victor began to protest. "But Mr. Renda..."

Domenico cut him off with a stern look, then, "When I say we go– WE GO NOW!"

Rowena and Victor once again carried Virginia quickly back to the car. Domenico was not far behind, carrying a double-barrel twelve-gauge shotgun. He sat in the back next to his daughter, assuring her everything would be fine. By the time they returned to the hospital, Domenico was whipped up into a fury. He bolted out of the car and jogged into the Emergency Room entrance. He began brandishing the 12-gauge madly as nurses and orderlies were ducking for cover.

"Who's the big boss? Where's the doctor who says my little girl can no come in?"

Nobody moved. After a moment, a doctor, in a white lab coat, walked briskly into the E.R. He was about to inquire as to why people were tucked behind desks, doors, and gurneys when he turned to face the business end of Domenico's shotgun.

"You gonna take my Virginia, give her a bed, and take care of her, yes?"

As Rowena and Victor entered with Virginia, they were shocked at the scene they walked into. The doctor looked at the teenager and knew she needed to be quarantined and attended to immediately.

"Of course, sir," was Doctor Grange's calm reply. He was tall and lean, his wide-set green eyes glowed in contrast to a full head of snow-white hair. "Please lower the rifle and we will give her the best treatment possible. Now, put the gun down so we can treat her. We certainly don't want to deal with any gunshot wounds, do we?"

Domenico looked around and for a moment, felt a twinge of embarrassment.

"No, no. Okay. But you take good care of her, doctor."

"You can count on it. Nurse Cranston, find this young lady a private room right away. We'll take care of the admitting paperwork later."

Nurse Cranston, a round, matronly woman, rose from behind a gurney. "Yes, doctor." She then looked to Victor. "Young man, please bring the girl over here and place her on the gurney."

Victor did as he was instructed and breathed a sigh of relief. Rowena looked around and followed him as he gently placed Virginia down on the rolling bed. They trailed Nurse Cranston and the gurney down the hallway with Domenico bringing up the rear, still cradling his shotgun.

The danger of fever-induced coma and permanent brain damage was imminent. The doctor ordered another nurse to find an orderly and have him begin chipping ice from a block and prepare an ice bath. As the teenager heard the doctor giving those instructions, she rolled back on the gurney and appeared to faint. The doctor began shouting at her, "NO! Do not sleep! Wake up!"

It was too late: Virginia was slipping into a coma. The doctor ordered a spinal tap to check the level of infection. A second nurse had just entered the room.

"Maureen, set me up for a spinal tap at once."

The nurse replied, "Do you want morphine for anesthesia?"

He thought for a moment. "No anesthesia." The nurse raised her eyebrows as he explained. "I'm hoping the discomfort will keep her conscious."

"Yes, doctor," Maureen said as she headed to the supply room.

Discomfort is an understatement. A spinal tap is a procedure where a long needle is placed in the spinal canal to extract some of the fluid for analysis. In the best of circumstances, it is a difficult procedure: First, the patient must be placed in the fetal position, curled up on one side. Next, a nurse (or nurses) must hold the patient in position while the needle is inserted. It can be challenging to find the right spot and can be extremely painful as the doctor searches for the spinal canal, even with anesthesia. The spine is made up of bones, which fit tightly together; below each spinal process, there is a hole, approximately half an inch in diameter in an adult. These are used as landmarks to find the general location of where to insert the needle. Once the location is decided upon, usually between the second and fourth lumbar, the needle is aimed toward the patient's belly button. If the right spot is hit, a nice steady flow of clear, colorless spinal fluid is the reward; a miss can result in a "bloody tap" and intense pain for the patient.

The doctor found the proper spot and began to insert the thick needle. Virginia moaned and began to squirm.

"Hold her still!" the doctor ordered. The two nurses were applying all the strength and weight they could muster on the young girl's body as the needle slowly made its way toward Virginia's spine.

That familiar feeling washed over her. Virginia looked around at the walls and ceiling becoming translucent. She could hear the doctor's shouts but they were muffled.

Peace; then the familiar, rushing sound of a locomotive as she was carried away at an incomprehensible speed. This time, she didn't have the opportunity to look back and see the events unfolding in the hospital; instead, Virginia's focus was on what was ahead of her. It was apparent that once again a destination lie ahead but she could only discern the quality of the atmosphere: Dark, chaotic, and frightening. She could feel evil surrounding her like a cold, heavy blanket. Beasts clawed at her, all the while they were swearing at her and cursing God. Virginia was in a place so dark she could not even see past her face. Even though she could not see the beasts, she intuitively knew exactly what they looked like: Tall, at least nine feet, scaly skin, and massive, clawed hands. The stench of sulphur, feces, death, and decay made her retch. If evil ever had a scent, this was it. Fear and a profound sense of isolation filled the young girl's mind until she realized that she was getting a glimpse of hell, a real place void of any single thing that humanity calls good. What cut the deepest was the separation from anyone or anything holy– God was nowhere in this place. She knew the beasts were approaching, about to tear her apart, only to knit her together to be torn apart again...over and over and over. They screamed obscenities, shouted about her worthlessness, that they possessed her wicked soul forever. She was horrified. That very moment, Virginia felt the need to cry out to the Lord; as the thought hit her tortured mind, she was whisked away on that rushing wind and her feelings shifted dramatically: Feelings of extreme contentment and peace. She heard the faint sound of singing, although it was hard to pinpoint if it was a song or a chorus. It was as if thousands of voices were raised up in worship, all singing differently; yet strangely, they blended into a glorious melody. It gave the impression that the heart and intention of each voice was what brought it into harmony with all the others.

The rushing stopped. All that remained were those beautiful harmonized voices. As she walked along a golden path, she heard more singing as though it was near her feet. On either side of the path, flowers of colors she had never seen before blossomed next to her. As each flower bloomed, it added its own voice to the beautiful choir of worship that surrounded her. She looked up and the sky was radiant, a mix of blues from indigo to cobalt to powder, with double and triple rainbows everywhere. Even the multi-colored arcs were singing "Holy, holy, holy". Virginia felt oneness, of belonging, like she had never experienced on earth. She continued to walk toward an intense yet inviting light; within she could see the form of someone very far away. With each step she was closer to being engulfed in the light, but the form, which radiated an even more powerful light of its own, remained at the same distance. Other vague light bodies were moving toward her and she knew they were people; not really people, but souls with perfect, glorified bodies. She marveled at the health and vibrancy each one radiated. As they came closer, she realized that she knew them... she knew them all, even if they had not met during her earthly lifetime There were relatives from ages past and friends of her mother and father's family ancestors. There was no dialogue but she clearly understood they were welcoming her to this destination. And somehow, this welcoming committee silently communicated that she had a review ahead of her; that the words and deeds of her young life were about to be played out. There was no movie screen, no projector, but Virginia sensed a mental playback about to start. Visual scenes, coupled with emotions, began to pour through her memory at an incredible speed. Flashes of her infancy, toddler, childhood, and early teen years blurred past yet contained a level of clarity more vivid than the actual experiences. Every word she spoke, entire conversations, moments both good and bad were on display. Virginia felt the joys and sorrows of these experiences with a deeper sense of emotion than she was capable of. Harsh words and thoughts from the past brought an extreme sense of remorse. Resentments and the times she disobeyed her parents were met with something that cut deeper than guilt. This rapid-fire accountability caused the young girl to respond with a profound sense of contrition, understanding how grave these errors were in her life. The rapidity of the review began to slow down as it closed in on her present age. The depth of her sorrow seemed inconsolable, heavy. As the mental movie came to an end, leaving Virginia staring at herself in the present day, an outpouring of love washed over her. It was warm like a blanket she could snuggle into. It felt like the love she had always craved from her father as a child. It wrapped around her and, at the same time, filled her. Revelation and wisdom filled her mind. She understood *metanoia*, repentance, and turned her full attention on Christ as He slowly approached the teen. The joy was overwhelming and she began to sob, tears of release from all the hurts given and received. As the waves of emotion ebbed, the profound peace that only comes with forgiveness settled upon her. The words "It is finished" echoed in her mind, and, as quickly, Jesus vanished from her vision as the rapid descent back to her body began. A voice inside said, "I am not ready for you yet– there is more for you to do."

The needle for a spinal tap procedure is large and hollow with a solid needle in the center, and a cap that holds the solid needle in its proper place. There are occasions when the needle will hit bone, in which case it must be removed and the painful process starts over. The doctor's touch was excellent and he found the space on the first try; however, due to the infection and high fever, the pressure of the spinal fluid was much higher than normal— so high that the cap holding the solid needle in place blew off as the doctor tried to remove it. Fortunately, there was enough fluid captured to make an accurate analysis.

Bulbar poliomyelitis is a serious form involving the medulla oblongata and usually becomes evident within three days. The muscles of swallowing and breathing are affected, so that the patient has difficulty swallowing, speaking, and breathing. In all forms, there may be subsequent atrophy of groups of muscles, ending in contraction, paralysis, and permanent deformity.

What struck Virginia first was that there was no physical pain like the first time she came back into her earthly frame after the scarlet fever. She opened her eyes and looked at the ceiling, looked around, then tried to sit up: She could not move her head;

89

as she tried to move her hand, it did not respond. Nothing from her feet or legs or arms or neck or body. The young girl began to panic and wanted to shout but even her vocal chords were paralyzed– the polio had done its damage.

Like most mammals, humans take in oxygen by a process called negative pressure breathing. The diaphragm contracts and the rib cage opens up. This expands the chest cavity and decreases the pressure in the chest, causing the lungs to fill with air. Then the diaphragm relaxes and the process reverses, causing exhalation. Most polio survivors suffer from paralysis of the diaphragm, making natural breathing impossible. The doctors assumed this and were all in agreement: Virginia would be placed inside a negative pressure ventilator for a minimum of one week. Also known as an iron lung, it is a metallic cylindrical chamber, which opens and closes lengthwise. The patient is placed inside from the neck down and the upper half of the cylinder is closed and locked, with only the head exposed. When it is sealed, it provides the proper atmospheric pressure cycles for a person to breathe without using their diaphragm, forcing air into the lungs through negative pressure and then forcing it out through adding pressure. If the young girl did not recover the use of her diaphragm with this therapy, she could anticipate being confined to the machine for the rest of her days.

There was something, however, the doctors had not taken into consideration: One of the side effects of Virginia's skill with a baritone horn was an over-developed diaphragm. And that, more than anything, most likely led to Virginia mustering up the will to rehabilitate herself as much as possible. The will to survive is inherent in all living creatures; the teenager focused all her attention on breathing. Sheer concentration caused Virginia's breathing rhythms to re-engage and within minutes, her breath was as normal as it had ever been. The doctors and nurses were astounded. After witnessing so many tragedies from polio, lost lives and lifeless bodies, it was truly a miracle to see this young woman breathing on her own so quickly.

At this point, the doctors were hesitant to make a definitive prognosis. Nonetheless, they informed Bessie that her daughter would not be able to have children due to the profound damage to Virginia's spinal cord. The nerves surrounding the spine were shut down and the disc cartilage had essentially collapsed. Her body would not be able to support a developing fetus through the process of childbirth. As far as walking or any other motor skills were concerned, that would be determined at a later time. For now, all were grateful that the young girl was capable of breathing– a very good sign.

After two weeks of observation in hospital, it was determined that Virginia would be best served going home. Aside from breathing, she had use of her retinal muscles and could "point" to things with her eyes. She was also learning to express herself more visually, smiling and thanking the hospital staff when they would feed her or tend to her needs. Domenico and Bessie arrived with Rowena to bring Virginia home. Bessie waited in the car while father and sister walked on either side of the girl being ushered out the front door by a nurse pushing the wheelchair. As they positioned Virginia in the back seat of the car, Bessie leaned over and reached out to touch her daughter's arm.

"We're so happy to have you home, Virginia."

Virginia was caught in a mix of emotions. A single tear rolled down her cheek. She could not feel the touch, she could not speak; part of her wanted to tell her mother about her heavenly experience and another part recalled the scolding Bessie gave her after the scarlet fever. Domenico called from the front door of the hospital– he needed help reading the discharge papers.

Bessie said, "Now sit tight, dear. I'll be right back and we'll all go home together."

Virginia wanted so badly to tell her mother where "Home" really was. As she was lying across the back seat, her head was propped up by the armrest on the passenger door behind the driver's seat. She looked down at her useless hand and thought, *You will move! You will heal!* She focused every ounce of thought and energy on her pinky finger. Nothing, then suddenly, a twitch. She forced her thoughts there again and the finger moved a little more. Once more and she could wiggle it! At that very moment,

Rowena slipped into the back seat as Domenico and Bessie got in the front. Nobody noticed Virginia's bug-eyed stare, moving her eyes toward her hand. She tried to speak but only air passed by her vocal chords; finally, she got Rowena's attention and "pointed" with her eyes at her hand.

Rowena shouted, "Mother! Father! Virginia is moving her little finger. Praise God, it's a miracle!"

Domenico and Bessie whirled around on the bench seat and looked back at their daughter.

"Sweet Jesus, Dom!" Bessie proclaimed.

Domenico looked at Virginia and began to weep and laugh simultaneously as he teased, "You gonna cause-a more trouble, little girl?"

Everyone broke into gales of laughter as Virginia smiled with her bright blue eyes. Domenico started the car, put it in gear, and they drove home to tell the other siblings the great news.

The road to recovery was long and, oftentimes, painful. Re-engaging muscles that had atrophied was arduous. One body part at a time, Virginia willed her body back into action. After she got her fingers moving on both hands, she began to work on the hands. Then the forearms. The upper arms. Shoulders. On some days, progress was made in a matter of hours; other times, it took days to get one motor skill back. Once she was able to sit up, Virginia decided she needed to cultivate an ability that would allow her to generate income and become more independent. With the passing of scarlet fever and the last incident of polio, Virginia had spent so much time exposed to doctors and nurses. She was fascinated with the medical profession. Her first thought was going to medical school but women doctors were unheard of at the time. Unfortunately, nursing required physical strength for moving patients and long hours. A friend had suggested she look into transcribing reports for doctors; with their scribbles and scrawls, physicians were always looking for someone to make sense of their notes on patients. Virginia convinced her father and mother that this was a good opportunity and they agreed.

CHAPTER 3. From Snow to Sand

1950 - 1960

Virginia's ability with a typewriter became newsworthy. At one point, she held the record for speed typing. It also captured the attention of a handsome young soldier with an adventuresome spirit.

Donald Isbell joined the Army to get an education. He was assigned to one of the most dangerous jobs as what is termed a "smoke jumper". These brave (and somewhat crazy) men parachute out of airplanes to land near blazing forest fires and commence battle with out-of-control infernos. Don courted Virginia while she was still rehabilitating her body but he didn't care about her limitations: He loved Ginger's independent spirit and flashing azure eyes.

Virginia rebuffed his proposals, telling Don that he would have to settle into a safe and steady career before she would consider marrying him. He knew God had a destiny for their lives and decided on pursuing a path as a schoolteacher. They were married in Washington State in October 1953 and made a home near Glacier

National Park in Kalispell, located in northwest Montana. David was their firstborn and Daniel came not long after.

One day, while bundling up the boys in their snowsuits on the front porch, Virginia turned away from Daniel to zip up David in his. When she turned back, Daniel was nowhere to be seen. She spied a faint patch of blue in the snowdrift in front of the porch. As she reached into the snow, she pulled out the suffocating boy who had turned as blue as his outfit! By the time Don had returned home from work that evening, Virginia told him she had had enough of snow and it was time to move.

Don's research of places to teach yielded three options: Florida, the territory of Guam, or the newly formed State of Hawaii. They agreed that Guam was too far from family, Florida was too hot and humid, and thus began preparing for a new life in the Aloha State.

When they arrived in Hilo, the town had recently been devastated by a tsunami. It was a rocky start but the locals took kindly to the Isbells. After Virginia gave birth to their third child, Mahealani, an elderly local Hawaiian woman showed up at their doorstep. Mrs. Ho'opai told her of a chronic eye disease she was suffering from and informed Virginia that breast milk was an ancient tribal cure. The mother of three was more than happy to provide for the elder Hawaiian based on one condition: Mrs. Ho'opai must teach the Hawaiian language to Virginia in exchange for her "medicine". The two became lifelong friends and Mrs. Ho'opai also gave Virginia instruction on Hawaiian herbal remedies and culture. Mrs.

Ho'opai would later become Godmother to the Isbell's fourth child, Iwalani.

CHAPTER 4. Another Day in Paradise

1963

Pahoa, Hawaii

Virginia was now thirty years old. She was pregnant with her fourth child and she knew the rhythms of pregnancy. The last couple days had been different, though. This sluggishness was unusual and a nagging ear and sinus infection would not clear up.

Don came home from teaching classes and called out to his wife. He found her in the bedroom, sleeping. It was a warm, humid afternoon; the rains had just subsided and the air felt thick. Virginia was tucked under the blankets. Sitting next to her on the bed, he reached out and gently touched her eight-month pregnant tummy.

He rubbed it gently as he spoke. "There's a double rainbow outside and the gardenias smell amazing." Then, in a concerned voice, "Is everything okay?"

"No, it's nothing, really," Virginia replied. "I'll be fine if I lie down for a little bit."

"Are you sure? Do you want to see the doctor?"

"No, really, Don. I'm fine. I'll get up and make dinner in just a minute."

By late afternoon, David and Daniel were home from after-school playtime with their friends. Two-year-old Mahealani had not been fed and Virginia felt too weak to get up and cook dinner. Don lightly placed the inside of his wrist against her forehead–she was burning with fever.

"Ginger, we're going to the hospital. Get up slowly and I'll walk you to the car."

Sally was the adopted *hanai* daughter of the Isbells. She came from Japanese heritage and was brutally abused as a child before Don and Virginia took her into their home. Don gave instructions to Sally to feed and take care of the children and took off for Hilo hospital. By the time they arrived, Virginia was tossing and turning in the front passenger seat, in a full body sweat with chills and aching everywhere. The ear and sinus infection had morphed into full-blown bacterial spinal meningitis.

Nicholas Steuermann graduated from medical school in Romania in 1937 with a promising future. His private practice as a dermatologist was interrupted when in 1942 the Nazis threw him into a concentration camp, where he spent the majority of the remainder of World War II. On Christmas Eve, 1944, a Russian platoon marched through the gates of the notorious prison; he was liberated from his captors, only to become a prisoner of the Russian Army for the next six months. He managed to escape and walked back to his village in Romania of 120,000 citizens. When he arrived home, he discovered that a mere two hundred souls were spared from the atrocities of the holocaust. Nicholas spent a few years helping other victims of that nightmare. Even after the war ended, many still succumbed to malnutrition, depression, and suicide; others lived with a profound sense of guilt that they had survived while others did not. Steuermann dedicated his life to helping others, not only through his medical practice but in other ways in the community, often anonymously. In the late 1940s, he was granted permission to immigrate to the United States. He made his way to Ohio and vowed to get as far away as possible from that hellhole he left behind in Eastern

Europe– and Hilo, Hawaii was literally on
the other side of the world.

Virginia's temperature was now 107°.
She was lapsing in and out of consciousness
as Don walked her into the hospital. At first,
the receiving nurse was going to place
Virginia in the maternity ward. As she was
calling for an orderly and wheelchair, Dr.
Steuermann noticed the pregnant woman
and her poor condition. He told the nurse to
place Virginia in quarantine until the proper
diagnosis was made. That one decision may

have prevented a pandemic with more lives lost. On the way to the private room, in a moment of lucidity, Virginia told Dr. Steuermann, "The baby is kicking... HARD!"

Dr. Steuermann looked over the rim of his spectacles, his Romanian accent still thick. "My dear, you vould be kicking too eef you vere svimming in boiling vater." They entered the room and he looked to the nurse standing just over his shoulder. "Ve vill haf need of a surgical kit. Prepare to do a Cesarean at once."

Virginia overheard the orders. "Doctor, if there is any way possible, I want to carry this baby to term. I am eight months along now and…"

The mother-to-be fainted as Dr. Steuermann made his way to the washbasin to prepare. He knew the child had little or no chance to survive under these conditions and getting it out as quickly as possible would minimize organ and brain damage as well as developmental problems from the mother's illness. The surgical team would have to act quickly to insure the infant's best chances.

It had been almost fifteen years but Virginia knew the feeling coming over her as if it were yesterday: The walls and ceiling melting away, a sense of peace as she detached from her body, and the ability to look at her surroundings. She could see the doctor standing over the basin, scrubbing his hands and forearms furiously with soap and water. As she rose higher, Virginia watched the nurse trotting down the hall, her heels echoing along the corridor. Nurse Jesse Campbell was new to Hilo Hospital. She and her husband had recently moved from Oregon to the Big Island where he worked as a welder for the local fishing boats in

Hilo harbor. Jesse entered the supply closet and pulled a sani-pack from the shelf, containing gear for minor surgery: scalpels, forceps, hemostats, sponges, etc. As she did, the sterilized linen cloth that held the instruments unwound. She managed to catch it but not before a scalpel hit the floor.

"Oh, shit," she exclaimed under her breath. The last thing she needed was a reprimand from her superior this early in her tenure at the hospital– Dr. Steuermann had a reputation for going by the book and being harsh toward his subordinates when an error was made. Jesse quickly grabbed the precision blade, wiped it on the sleeve of her uniform, and rolled the linen back to its original setting. She hurried back to the room, ready to assist in delivering the baby.

Virginia felt a sense of urgency hit. Her main concern as she saw Nurse Jesse entering the operating room was that a dirty scalpel could be catastrophic. One wrong slip of the blade and infection would kill her unborn child. The euphoria left as she willed herself from rising any further, commanding her spirit body to return to its physical residence. Heaven would just have to wait.

Virginia's next conscious thought was of pain: Pain from breathing, pain from lying in the hospital bed, pain from thinking. She was back in her body and it felt heavy, cumbersome. The mother-to-be moved her hands to her belly, feeling the unborn child's form just beneath her skin. Relief, then sleep.

The next time she woke, Virginia was lying on her right side. Slowly opening her eyes, she looked into the hallway of the hospital just outside her door. She heard footsteps, obviously female, judging by the *clack-clack* of the heels on the terrazzo floor. A nurse was passing by her room and Virginia immediately recognized the woman. She lifted a finger and pointed to the nurse, saying in a soft, weak voice, "I know you!"

The woman in uniform stopped cold, looking at the pregnant mother in bed. "I don't believe you do, ma'am," was her reply.

"I saw you walking in the hallway. I saw you in the closet. I saw you drop the instruments. I heard you say, 'Oh, shit.' And I saw you running back to the surgery."

Nurse Jesse was dumbstruck. She felt chills through her entire body as her face went sheet-white. The churning in her stomach brought a wave of nausea. She tried to speak but could only muster a stuttering, "I-I-I..." as an apology before staggering away.

Virginia closed her eyes again, thanking God for the gift of being able to bring her fourth child into the world. Serenity erased her cares and worry as she faded into a dreamless slumber.

EPILOGUE

In the mid-1960s, the Isbell *ohana* moved to the other side of the Big Island and settled in the historic town of Kealakekua, where they had their fifth child, Richard Ka'eo. . Don continued teaching at Konawaena High School and Virginia expanded her career as a public servant– Girl Scout leadership, swimming & water safety instructor, and much more. She went on to spend fourteen years in the Hawaii State House of Representatives followed by six years as a County Councilwoman.

I first met Virginia Isbell in October 2003 when I was courting her daughter Iwalani. She and her husband Don were about to celebrate their fiftieth anniversary and they made a family reunion out of the occasion. Friends and relatives from neighboring Hawaiian Islands, the mainland, and other countries showed up for the celebration. It was on the eve of that milestone that I found myself in a Chinese restaurant on the Big Island, sitting next to this snowy-haired pistol of a woman.

Exactly one year and a day later, on their fifty-first anniversary, Virginia and Don stood next to Iwalani and me on the beach as we exchanged our wedding vows. You could see the motherly pride and the joy she felt that her daughter was happy and in love.

Over the years, Virginia and I have developed a loving, respectful relationship. Like most mothers- and sons-in-law, we have had our moments of head-butting and disagreements, always to forgive one another. I tell people 'I have an amazing wife and got a great mother-in-law thrown into the deal!" I am in awe of what this intelligent, driven woman has overcome and achieved. She has taken life situations that many would consider impossible and turned them around for the good. In the political arena, Virginia has always been considered one of the "good ones", with a record of impressive accomplishments, ranging from initiating recycling programs to creating affordable housing for native Hawaiians. She has given free piano lessons to hundreds of children in Hawaii. Everything she has put her hand to has been fruitful: Blowing a horn in the orchestra or a conch shell at momentous events; being a steerswoman on a Hawaiian canoe; participating in team triathlons in her late-seventies. Her can-do attitude coupled with a quirky rebellious streak is a powerful one-two punch. After her polio episode, the doctors said she would never be able to have children– she had five. Her four surviving children (her second son Daniel is home with the Lord) are successful in their respective businesses and have rich family lives. Virginia's legacy is an example of what an empowered woman can create when one seeks the opportunities God places before them. And she has blessed many others by what she has given back.

Jesus commanded us to love one another. Virginia Isbell has led a life aligned with that mandate. She jokingly says that she is a three-time reject of Heaven but anyone who knows her can tell you that God has had an enormous calling and purpose for her life… or maybe Heaven wasn't quite ready for her!

May we all love and serve as Virginia has.

AFTERWORD

Everyone I am associated with knows me as a "take me as I am" person. The only instances I have made compromises is when it came time to get things done in politics...but I never compromised my principles, values, or character. You may or may not believe what is written in this book, but these experiences are the way I recall how it happened.

I was approached many years ago to discuss these moments in my life but never felt comfortable doing so– until now. Most of these memories were suppressed for a long time. When I nearly died with scarlet fever and later with polio, my mother warned me against speaking about them; that people would think I was involved in sorcery, witchcraft, or just plumb crazy. After recovering from spinal meningitis, I discussed all three incidents with my husband Don, who was very supportive.

Recalling these events not only brought up the intensity of the experiences, it also renewed the anger and frustration I felt toward being forced to stay quiet about something that, I felt, was of major importance. As a young girl, that oppression fueled my rebellious streak. I suppose it served me in some ways in my career as a politician as well as bucking trends as a parent. I told all my children they were capable of doing anything they put their minds to and to never let anyone limit their dreams. Ultimately, reliving all of this allowed me to come to terms with old emotions, forgive, and understand that my mother was doing what mothers are hard-wired to do: Protect their children at all cost.

It is my hope that by revealing these experiences, you will find value in them. Perhaps you had a similar encounter; maybe you know someone who came close to death, yet never understood what truly happened to them in the process. Personally, they left me with a knowing that there is more to life than what we see, touch, taste, smell, and hear. Whatever path you walk in faith, I am here (still!) to tell you that I've had a glimpse of Heaven, that there is a God who loves us, that there is *something* after we leave this earthly plane.

Let that fill your spirit and give you peace.

-Virginia Isbell

ABOUT THE AUTHOR

Gordon Noice is a Florida native, surfer, ordained minister, and has an extensive background in theatre, film and television. His unique style of speaking and message of encouragement & empowerment are well received wherever he travels. Gordon lives in Hawaii with his wife Iwalani.

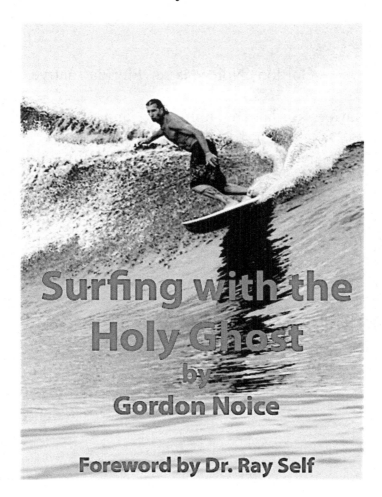

Surfing with the
Holy Ghost
by
Gordon Noice

Foreword by Dr. Ray Self

OTHER TITLES by GORDON NOICE

THE LAST LAUGH IS FREE

LIFER

Gordon Noice

NOTES

90277453R00078

Made in the USA
Columbia, SC
01 March 2018